WEATHERED
THE STORM

WEATHERED
THE STORM

Derek A. Chandler

AuthorHouse™ LLC
1663 Liberty Drive
Bloomington, IN 47403
www.authorhouse.com
Phone: 1-800-839-8640

Published by AuthorHouse 02/17/2014

ISBN: 978-1-4918-6365-7 (sc)
ISBN: 978-1-4918-6435-7 (e)

Library of Congress Control Number: 2014902994

Contents

A New Days Dawning

I did not want to wake up today
To face all this pain
I am feeling inside
There are moments when I would trade all this pain
Just to die
Who knows how cold my soul
Has begun to get inside
I face this world
With a hurtful set of eyes
A heavy heart full of sorrow
A very dark and gloomy outsight
Of any tranquil tomorrows
Inside my heart I've cried
Inside my heart I've died
Now what more
Do I do to stay alive
Inside I feel it is a fight lost
Cause somewhere down in my chest
I feel I even loss
My sense of pride
Maybe this is finally
When I arrive at the point
In my life
When all the hurt is
Put to a rest

P.S. Thank you Lord for having this discussion I think I arrived at the point in my life where the pain is put to rest thanks truly God Bless

Boy Blue

Who cared about a boy
Named blue
Who cared if they knew
Who cared if he ever saw
Tomorrow
Who cared to even let him
Borrow
All he wanted to borrow
Was someone's heart
Because the one he was given
Was broken from the start
But he remained strong
In heart, soul and mind
Even though he
Never got to see
Who would open their
Heart shaped door
Who would care
For a little boy
Named blue
Whose heart
Always remined torn and
Yearned for more

Broken Man Inside a Broken Home

A broken home is the reason I'm alone
Broken homes before and since the day I was conceived
I'm figuring is the reason
Why my world is the way it seems to be
Never letting the inner beauty of myself be seen
To many times I tried
But ended up with the same conclusion why I cry
A broken home Is all I've known
When is the day going to come
When I feel I'm not going to run from a normal home
Life is all I ask
When will this broken life come to past

A New Days Dawning

I did not want to wake up today
To face all this pain
I am feeling inside
There are moments when I would trade all this pain
Just to die
Who knows how cold my soul
Has begun to get inside
I face this world
With a hurtful set of eyes
A heavy heart full of sorrow
A very dark and gloomy outsight
Of any tranquil tomorrows
Inside my heart I've cried
Inside my heart I've died
Now what more
Do I do to stay alive
Inside I feel it is a fight lost
Cause somewhere down in my chest
I feel I even loss
My sense of pride
Maybe this is for the best
Maybe this is finally
When I arrive at the point
In my life
When all the hurt is
Put to a rest

P.S. Thank you Lord for having this discussion I
think I arrived at the point in my life where the
pain is put to rest thanks truly and God Bless

Child of the Ghetto

Child of the ghetto
Please say goodnight
Don't let your eyes fill with tears
Let go of all your childhood fears
Do not cry maybe this will be the night
Mom and dad don't hit the pipe
Do not worry about being left all alone at home
Mom will enter the room and tuck you
Into a warm bed tonight
Kissing you softly on your forehead
And wishing you a goodnight
So lay your burdens down
And say a prayer to the heavenly father above
Hold on tight
Because there's no reason or need
To be full of fright
Dad will also be there to turn off your light
So please lay your head down
Let go of all your sorrow
Realizing there is hope for brighter and better
Tomorrows
You may let out a sigh of relief
Cause tonight you will not have to feel the grief
Or fright behind your door
About the sight of Mom and Dad in another domestic fight
Do not toss, turn or shake
From your case of bad nerves
Once you awake from your nightmare
Better believe you will have from this life what you deserve
Let your eyes get heavy and I wish you goodnight
Child of the ghetto
Do not worry about the outside of your window full of screams
Cause once you awake
The ghetto will not have a hold on your dreams

<u>Every Rose Has A Thorn</u>

Do you want to know why
I sometime breakdown and cry
Cause deep down inside
I know how it feels
During trying times to survive

Sometimes I cry and come to the realization why
Because I guess the hurt I've felt inside
Has come to the point
Where it has withered and died

Put to rest, put to the test, put to the side
The most dangerous or detrimental
Part of my internal growth
The thorn in my side
My sense of pride

Family Ties that Bind

Family ties can make you cry
Maybe even make you bubble inside
Might also be the reason why
Your heart has died
Maybe you been lost on the inside
Because you have been robbed blind
Of one of the most greatest virtues alive
Which in turns builds strength and pride
Your family ties

Foster Child and Abandoned Ones

I realize and I know
Life is a lot harder for you son
Can you find it in your heart
To please forgive this world
For what we have done
We seldom see your need
And have not started
To give you
The time you need to heal
From all the open wounds
Your tender heart has always felt
I know you feel
Isolated and alone
In a world that can
Sometimes feel as cold as stone
You are defenceless and vulnerable
As a grain of desert sand
Somewhere far off in a distant land

Four Quiet Corners

Stuck in the four corners of my soul
Knowing I went down
Every road to finally
Be stuck at the fork
Of the road in my soul
Now which way do I turn
To cease this pain that is all so real
During the quiet times
Is when I hear the loudness
And feel the strength of this pain
I try to numb this feeling with a masked emotion
I've turned cold inside
Knowing each day a part of my soul dies

I Never Cried Like I Cried Today

I never cried like I cried today
I heard one man say
Out of all the simple joy in life
He has not one to cherish
No one cares to lend
His fears an ear
He says he has been
Here and there
To un-turn every stone
To find nothing there but despair
That when I told the man
I never cried like I cried today
Cause there are moments
In my life
When I've felt
The same way

Lonely Mans Voice

I've cried tears for so many years
I've cried tears out of fear
I've cried tears because life's grief's were to hard to bear
I've cried tears because life's serenity came to share
I've cried tears the day god answered my prayers
I've felt the pain of the man who cried
I've seen how this pain has become to make tearful eyes
I've had a long journey down the road called life
I've to been dealt a hand called gods strife

In my Shadow Part Two

In my shadow
You shall see
All the ill's of my life
Once I became to be
In my shadow
You shall see
A lonely child
Whose heart bleeds
In my shadow
You shall see
A distant man
Torn by his reality
In my shadow
I shall
Travel all alone
With only the depths of the chains
Put upon my soul
In my shadow
I will realize
That life will sometimes
Come from the blind side
Hidden in the form of disguise
In my shadow
Your heart shall bleed
Because one life is all I lead
In my shadow I travel alone
Throughout the depths
Of solitude with chains
Put upon my soul
In my shadow
You shall see
Where the sun has sometimes shone
In my path travelled alone
In my shadow

I hope you shall learn to live because
In my shadow
One life is all I had to give
In my shadow
You shall see
An angel break the chains
You put upon me
In my shadow
I shall pour out my soul
Leaving nothing behind
Except for the chains
You put on my soul

In My Shadow

In my shadow
You shall see
All the pain that has become me
In my shadow
You shall see
An angel that was born to lead
In my shadow
You shall see
Pain and suffering
That should be
Turned to glee
In my shadow
You will see
A little boy
That cried to find a spot to be
In my shadow
You will see
A young man
That cried to be
free

It's Raining Tears Tonight

Please girl don't shed a tear
You know how much I always cared
If anything you know I will always
Be there
To erase all your fears
I will make sure there is nothing to fill
Your heart with despair
As you lay down my angel
Weeping and crying
For a better life tonight
Just began to imagine the thought
Of me and you together
Living in a miraculous world
As husband and wife
Would this be enough
To erase all the fears
You have faced throughout
These painful years
Maybe I'll be able
To help you face the fright
Of all these long
Cold lonely nights
Just imagine my tender touch
Never have I loved
A woman as much
I'll wipe the tears you cry
Dry from your set of sorrowful eyes
With a warm touch
You're the only woman
I've become to lust
What would you do if I said
I only want to share my life
With you
If I were to tell you
You're the only lady

I adore
Would you open your heart
Shaped door
And take
My heart as a token of my affection
Trust in me lady that you will
Never be neglected
If there is one thing
I've wanted out of this life
It would be for you to
Take my hand
And say
I will be your wife

Left Alone

Now I know
I was meant to die alone
How I know this is because
My heart has been empty
And never had a home
I wish I never walked
Through life in solitude
I've seen flashes of humanity
Then on the other hand
I noticed lots of human insanity
That's why I hope this comes to an end
Because I feel as though I have no friend
But my shadow
Don't cry just realize
I was born to die
On my own
I will leave this earth alone

Life and Times

Life will you show me that
You care
Life will you show me you hear
My prayers
Times when I'm suffering
Will I be able to deal with my life
Times when I'm alone will I be comforted
By life
The life and times
Of a young man that had
Times in his life when he
Couldn't stand

Life's Roads and Signs

I read the signs that lay ahead
But chose to pass them
Realizing one day to myself
That these signs I read
May lead to the difference of me
Staying alive or winding up in a disaster
Only the Lord will be able to slow me down
In a traffic jam we call life
How I know I just past around a corner
Where life has been full of strife
Taking my first left on Depression Ave.
Hoping not to end up in sadness Lane
I try to pull a u-turn but end up re-living the pain
I then took a right
With the hope to meet up with
My Lord the savior on guiding light
He had just left another pedestrian said
Just follow the road throughout the night
Until your soul begins to feel right
So I kept pushing thoughout the
Gravely fog of the night
Until I chose between the fork in the orad
Which read to the right
If you chose to follow me
You will have eternal life
Because I no longer wanted to feel pain
And wanted God to be part of my life
In a steady pace I headed down right
Until I reached the heavenly gates
Called Eternal Life
Out front the Lord was waiting saying
Please welcome me in your life
Because I no longer want you to feel
The bumpy roads of
Life's strife

Look Down and Hear my Heavenly Prayer

My mother there is so much
I would like to say to you tonight
This is the reason why I'm kneeled
On both my knees and praying
To you about our life
I never meant your life to be full of strain
Please forgive me and ignore all
The ignorance of my childhood pain
Let the lord know how much
I've creid since you died
Or O' so suddenly passed onto eternal life
My mother I know I've been the cause
Of the storm inside your life
But please realize at the end of my life
I'm expecting everything to turn out alright
I'm hoping you can make it rhough
All the rainy nights
Which were caused by all the hurt and pain
I brought you in this life
But please hold on and acknowlesge
My prayers tonight
Never giving up on
The hope and faith of us
Having a better life

My Dearest friend

My dearest friend
Where have you been
I miss you very dearly
You always been
That very near and special friend
A beautiful blend
Of companion, intimacy and devotion
Together throughout our lives
We shared so much deep emotion
Always there in my time of need
Always knowing when my heart would bleed
I've been missing you for O' so long
When can I come back home
To where I belong
To your warm embrace and
Your tender touch with all my heart I felt lust
Which was as sharp
As the dart cupid shot
Through my heart
I loved you O' so long
You're as sweet as the music from the strings
Of a beautiful harped song
My dearest friend
I been missing you since you been gone
I was not aware of how much you still cared
I hope you don't feel alone
And feel as much fear as me my friend
I hope we can start this over
Were we began
Hope this never has to come to an end
Love you wish all the fire and passion
From the pit of my heart
Lets reconcile and
Rekindle this flame to its start
Only the lord knows how much

I hope you remain
Until the end
Your one and only
Dearest Friend

My Prayer

Whatever you lose
Please don't lose your tools
The ones that have been given to you
By the grace of God
If you do not make it through the last night
Always remember your try and your valid fight
If you come back and some see your way through again
Remember not to get caught up
In all the world winds
And if you resurrect and some how get to see Christ
Remember he is your only guiding light
And when death comes to your door
Remember you gave your heart to the Lord
Only the Lord will guide you through all the pastures
You must remember that they will not only be green
But of many different colors and textures
With the hope that he is the light
You look deep down inside for the fight
When you have the chance to breath again
You show the world
The fight and loss
A real man goes though
But always remember that there is plenty to lose
Which is why you always play with your heart
That is the only thing some say will keep you smart
Just remember to always love
And that will be enough to keep you smart
Just remember to always love
And that will be enough to keep you above
All the waters and rainfalls in your life
When you drown in pain
Always remember to give your all
If everything in this life crippled you
Which sometimes made you feel small
Look in your heart and

Remember you loved and gave your all
But for now
So long and say goodnight
And remember with your mind
How your heart gave you the best fight
And you will always make it through the darkest night

My Truest Friend

My truest friend where have you been
Since you been gone
My heart no longer feels
As though it has a place
Where it belongs
Every passing second
Not by your side
My soul feels as though it has died
Since we've been apart
I no longer feel the beat of two
Intimate hearts
Please my friend
I would like to know
If we could go back to where we bagan
Instead of this bitter end
Tell me why we would depart
When we knew the love we had for each other
In the bottom of our hearts
My friend I am now feeling alone
I feel as though I no longer have
That special place in the corner of your heart
That I can call home
Tell me my friend
When can I come and see
You again
Love you always
Your one and only
Truest friend

No Questions Asked

There are no questions that will ever have to be asked
I hope our love will forever last
The last time I had you on my mind
Was the last time I seen twinkle in the sky
The rain and comets fell from the heavens above
The lord let me know you were the only lady I've been wishing of
Similar to the last drop borrowed from a penniless wishing well
To the last time you cast your ancient spell
Until the end of time, I'm hoping and praying your heart will forever remain mine
You've cast the most unforgettable spell
Now I'm the one who possesses the most riches
placed in my penniless wishing well

Nurture My Seed

God please take care of my seed
The one I regret I will be unable to see
Until I reach heaven or thy
My son my first unborn
And only one
I swear I did truly care
With a darkened heart I now cry many tears
I wanted you to be O'so very near
May my child be able to hear my prayers
Please lord cover him with your hands
In your holy covenant take care
And nurture this seed of misfortune
We have come to the realization that
This life was taken for no importance
So for now my child
I bid thy farewell
I will be there in a while
Please for the sake of the lord
Maintain your smile
Love you forever
My first aborted child

Stood Alone

Remember when you use to stand alone
And wonder who was going to walk you home
I remember when I stood alone
And had no one to walk me home
I remember not wanting to open the door
Cause nothing was behind it to take me home
And when I would take my first step and walk into the cold
That's when I realized I was alone
But living in another lonely woman's home
Who's heart was broken by grief and sorrow
But she always knew if she stayed strong
She would see another tomorrow

Tears

I cried tears
For so many years
I cried tears out of fear
I cried tears because I
Was unable to share life's grief;s
I cried tears in the dark
When I was screaming to God
To help me find my heart
I cried tears when I did not know where to start
I cried tears when I lost hope
I cried tears when God answered my prayers
I cried tears because life's
Serenity's came to share
I cried tears
When the lord showed me
How much he adored and cared
I cried tears

Thank you

Thank you my heavenly father
For hearing what I have to say
Thank my lord for giving me another day
Thank you Jesus for giving me reasons to pray
Because if I never had you to carry me
Through the valleys and peaks
I might not be here today

P.S. I know I've come a long way. My life has been an
experience. A positive change from day to day. I wish
I could change the past but that is not a reality

The Day We Fell Apart

The day we fell apart
Is the day we broke cupid's heart
The day we fell apart
There was no longer an arch in cupid's arc
The day we fell apart we shot the spark
Out of cupid's heart
The day we fell apart cupid cried
Because he knew the strong force of our love
Should not subside
The day we fell apart
Was the day we broke cupids heart

Untitiled

Can my life be turned around
Because I am feeling myself
Slowly beginning to touch ground
Of all the great things
I could have done with my life
I have slowly begun to feel Gods strife
I have vision myself in
The most wonderful places
Now all I can feel or see
Is these void spaces
Please bring forth
A more beautiful day
So somehow I can find
A way to see
A reasonable way
Down this road
Which I call strife
Because I really want God
To become part of my life
Please God steer me
In the right direction
I understand whatever way
You choose for me
Is at your own discretion
As I stand alone feeling as cold
As desert sand after the sun has shone
The eye of a storm
Isolated at the end
Of life's whirlwinds

Untitled

Who cared about a father
That could not bother to stand
Who cared about a man that you would
Sometimes yearn to hear holler
Who cared about a man that was always gone
He is the same man
That stood you up in the cold
And you did not have a place in his heart of your own
You truly never understood
Why he left home leaving you all alone
But every night before you would go to sleep
You would cry and plead
Please come home and see
What kind a man
I have grown to be
Who is a man who deserted his son
Who is a man who abandoned his daughter
The same man that was left by his father
Who is a man with one
True regret
He is a man his children
Try to forget

Walk Alone

When you feel alone and
You have no home
And you can't find a heart
You look in a place that you think is dark and
Your answers sometimes lie and
You feel like you want to let out a cry
But it doesn't matter you already died
Over and over inside

Weathering the Storm

You tell me you will be alone
Because you have felt the depths of life's colds
You possess so many wonderful qualities
How can somebody like you feel
There's no happy tomorrows
Don't say life will be your largest disappointment
Use life's ills as your healing ointment
Please do not let the warmth
You possess inside come to
The point where it finally subsides
Try to heal the aches of
Your empty chest and put your
Sadness to rest
I feel all the pain you internally
Push to the side
Please let go and try to
Expereince how and why
It may feel and be important to
Sometimes cry
Just realize that there still is pleasure
During life's stormy weathers
And if you weather this storm
You will find you possess
So many hidden treasures

P.S. Dedicated to the heartbroken and troubled minds and hearts that feel the depths of life's weathers. Just remember that you can always experience Pleasure during life's stormy weathers and if you can weather this storm you will realize you possess so many hidden treasures when faced with life's stormy weathers

What About a Father

What about a father
That left his daughter
What about a father
That you would sometimes
Yearn to hear holler
What about a father
That could not bother
What about a father
That you knew you would
Not see tomorrow
What about a father
Who did not teach right or wrong
What about a man
That was always gone

What about the Kids

What about the kids
That died in the war
What about the kids
That didn't care if they were poor
What about the kids
That didn't care if they died
What about the kids
That just needed their health to stay alive
What about all the sick children around the world
Who cared if they were alone
Who cared if they ever found a home
Who cared if they walked with God
Who cared to see them cry
Who do you think cared for their health
Jesus walked with them
On their dying days
God walked them too
During those days
That is what kept
The kids alive during their wars
He is all they needed
To keep their hearts
Warm

What's His Name

What's a man with no heart
He is a man that can't give his
Son and daughter
A real true start
What's a man with no cares
He is a father that was never there
What's a man with cold blood
He is a man that abandoned his son
What's a man that could not bother
He is the same man that
Adandoned his daughter
What's a man with one true regret
He is a man his children forget

When your souls Universe is complete

When the soul is complete
Everything in that souls universe
Becomes unique
Even when you lose sleep
And you see all the worlds sorrows
Your heart begins to cry
For tranquil tomorrow's
Some where down the line
You want to begin to cry
Because you finally found your relief
From all of life;s grief;s
You realize all this time
You hurt your mind
Because you were walking blind
Find your world and then
Never let it go
Because peaceful times may come
And go

When the Rain falls

The rain falling across
My window pane is a
Sudden and slow reminder
Of lives lost in wars
Of children who died
Because they were poor
Of couples who lost
Love for each one
Of a mother who lost a son
On a dark lonely cold road
To a world full of hate
But when the rain falls
That's the time god is
Feeling the pain of
All

When you Smile and the World Doesn't Smile Back

When you try to smile and the world
Doesn't smile back you may feel
As though you are about
To crack as though you are laying flat
You try to counter attack
But can't help to remember
They locked you in a world
That won't smile back you want to
Laugh and some times play
But will you ever get the chance
To say what you truly wanted to say
Always remember that the world won't always smile back
But remember to give a real counter attack
If you stand and your sometimes alone
Remember to never sell your soul
That's when the world won't smile back
Then you really won't be left with no counter attack
That's how gruesome it can
Get when the world won't smile back

Who Cared About

Who cared about a father
Who made him fend for himself
Who cared about a father
Who left him all by himself
Who cared if you seen him another day
Who cared if he walked out
Remember all the disbelief
Because he always lied
That's what always kept
All your anger
Bottled
Inside

You Don't Need a Hand

You don't need a hand
To smile
It only cost a nominal fee
To smile
A lot of time is usually free
To walk
Across a cloud
You sometimes want to try
But all the negatives
Make you want to die
Then you don't know
Who locked you inside
The corner of your heart
That's when you remember
You've been torn
From the very start

You May Blossom

Never let the sign
Of a cloud in the sky get you down
Cause the sun will always shine through again
You will experience many
Rainfalls in your lifetime
But you must always
Remember that these temporary
Showers will always bloom flowers
And that this rain has fell upon your life
All for a reason it's because
You are becoming seasoned
So after the temporary shower
You may look in the distant sky
And feel the glow of some of
The most beautiful visions
Of life's colourful rainbows
So whatever you do maintain a smile
Because the temporary showers
You will experience in life
Will only last a short while
These showers always bloom flowers
And you will experience these
Small rainstorms in your lifetime
For a reason its because you are
Experiencing life's seasons
Which is all a matter
Of your personnel growth
So weather the storm
So the seeds you plant
Along life's paths
May grow

P.S. It's all for a reason you are becoming seasoned

You Thought You Will Never See Another Day

You thought
You would never see another day
But you still seen
You walked through the dark night
All you seen was disbelief
You walked and walked on
And your heart tried to remain strong
Everything made you feel like you couldn't go on
But that's how the world is
When you feel you don't belong
Sometimes when you sing out beautiful songs
The world still tends to think
You were miserable all along

A Mothers Gone But Still She Lives On In Your Heart

Remember when you wanted to talk to your mother
and she was floating on a cloud
and you knew you weren't aloud
to come between all of heavens peace
but you always believed she was alive
and you kept her love locked inside
you held the key to all her dreams
and one day you told her
you'll see all these things
come to be

I Never Want To Feel Pain No More

I never meant to cause pain
I always meant to come again
I always knew right from wrong
I always knew it wouldn't be long
I always knew the key to life
I never wanted to feel Gods strife
The pain I feel
when I beat on his door
Is a pain
I don't want to feel no more

Life and Times

Life will you show me that you care
Life will you show me you hear my prayers
Times when I'm suffering will I be able to deal with my life
Times when I'm alone will I be comforted by life
The life and times of a young man
that had times in his life
when he couldn't
stand

Love

They say love comes
from the heavens above
But you remember
some nights still
get as cold as December
And you still see
that autumn leaves still fall off trees
And you still know
that the sand in the desert
is still cold
when it stands alone
Sometime you'll see
that spring will bring breeze
and when you look for change
remember to stay sane
and that's when your love
will come again

What's His Name

What's a man with no heart
he is a man that cant give his
son and daughter
a real true start
What's a man with no cares
he is a father that was never there
What's a man with cold blood
he is a man that abandoned his son
What's a man that could not bother
he is the same man that
abandoned his daughter
What's a man with one true regret
he is a man his children forget

Take A Walk

Take a walk with god he will give you light
Take a walk with God he will keep you right
Take a walk with God he will help you keep the faith
Take a walk with God there will never be a void space
Take a walk with God he will keep you safe
Take a walk with God he will let you see all the children's face

Closed Doors

A closed mind can create
delusions and figments
of your mind to
hallucinate at times
But imagination can heal wounds
and take away sorrow
so there will be many tomorrows
lost souls can make
the night go cold
yet there will be
another day that
will bring forth pain
my mind gets in a twist
which causes my
whole earth to flip

Stood Alone

Remember when you stood alone
and wondered who was gonna walk you home
I remember when I stood alone
And had no one to walk me home
I remember not wanting to
open the door because nothing was
behind it to take me home
And when I would take my
first step and
walk in the cold
that's when I would remember
there's no one to talk to
at home
That's when
I realized I was alone
but living in
another lonely woman's home whose heart was broken by
grief and sorrow
but she always knew if
she stayed strong she would see another tomorrow

Printed in the United States
By Bookmasters